AF228347

Lerner SPORTS

MEET
VLADIMIR GUERRERO JR.

DAVID STABLER

Lerner Publications ◆ Minneapolis

Copyright © 2023 by Lerner Publishing Group, Inc.

All rights reserved. International copyright secured. No part of this book may be reproduced, stored in a retrieval system, or transmitted in any form or by any means—electronic, mechanical, photocopying, recording, or otherwise—without the prior written permission of Lerner Publishing Group, Inc., except for the inclusion of brief quotations in an acknowledged review.

Lerner Publications Company
An imprint of Lerner Publishing Group, Inc.
241 First Avenue North
Minneapolis, MN 55401 USA

For reading levels and more information, look up this title at www.lernerbooks.com.

Main body text set in Aptifer Slab LT Pro. Typeface provided by Linotype AG.

Editor: Lauren Foley

Library of Congress Cataloging-in-Publication Data

Names: Stabler, David author.
Title: Meet Vladimir Guerrero Jr. / David Stabler.
Description: Minneapolis, MN : Lerner Publications , [2023] | Series: Sports VIPs (Lerner Sports) | Includes bibliographical references and index. | Audience: Ages 7–11 years | Audience: Grades 2–3 | Summary: "First baseman Vladimir Guerrero Jr. of the Toronto Blue Jays is one of baseball's most powerful sluggers. He broke a home run record in the 2019 Home Run Derby. Readers will thrill to learn about this baseball superstar"— Provided by publisher.
Identifiers: LCCN 2021055001 (print) | LCCN 2021055002 (ebook) | ISBN 9781728458243 (Library Binding) | ISBN 9781728463384 (Paperback) | ISBN 9781728462240 (eBook)
Subjects: LCSH: Guerrero, Vladimir, 1999– —Juvenile literature, | Baseball players—Canada—Biography—Juvenile literature. | Toronto Blue Jays (Baseball team)—History—Juvenile literature. | All-Star Baseball Game—History—Juvenile literature. | Fathers and sons—Juvenile literature.
Classification: LCC GV865.G84 S73 2023 (print) | LCC GV865.G84 (ebook) | DDC 796.357092 [B]—dc23/eng/20220225

LC record available at https://lccn.loc.gov/2021055001
LC ebook record available at https://lccn.loc.gov/2021055002

Manufactured in the United States of America
1-50854-50191-7/7/2022

TABLE OF CONTENTS

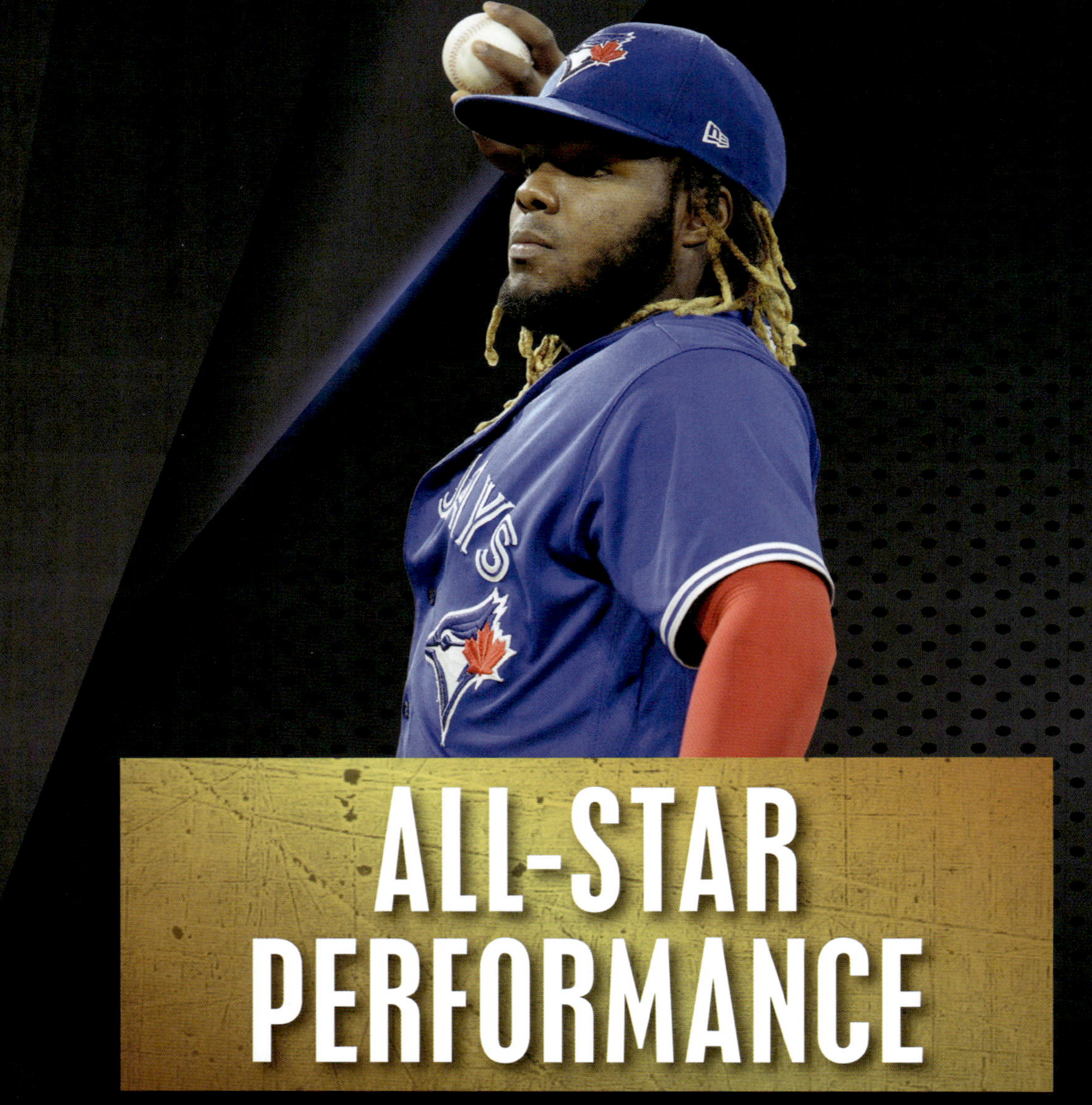

ALL-STAR PERFORMANCE

Vladimir Guerrero Jr. hit a home run for the ages. On July 13, 2021, the 22-year-old stepped up to the plate in the third inning of the All-Star Game. The annual game took place at Coors Field in Denver, Colorado. Guerrero's American League (AL) team led 1–0. The Toronto Blue Jays first baseman wanted to leave his mark on the game.

With two batters out and no one on base, Milwaukee Brewers pitcher Corbin Burnes threw the ball. *Bam!* Guerrero slammed the pitch deep into the outfield stands. The incredible moon shot measured 468 feet (143 m). It was the longest All-Star Game home run

FAST FACTS

DATE OF BIRTH: March 16, 1999
POSITION: first base and third base
LEAGUE: Major League Baseball (MLB)

PROFESSIONAL HIGHLIGHTS: played in the 2021 All-Star Game; led MLB in home runs in 2021; was the youngest Blue Jays player ever to hit a home run

PERSONAL HIGHLIGHTS: is the son of Baseball Hall of Famer Vladimir Guerrero Sr.; is the nephew of former MLB player Wilton Guerrero; grew up in Canada, the US, and the Dominican Republic

ever recorded. Guerrero's homer put the AL ahead for good 2–0.

Guerrero's Blue Jays teammates Bo Bichette and Teoscar Hernández were the first players to welcome him back to the AL dugout. The home run was extra

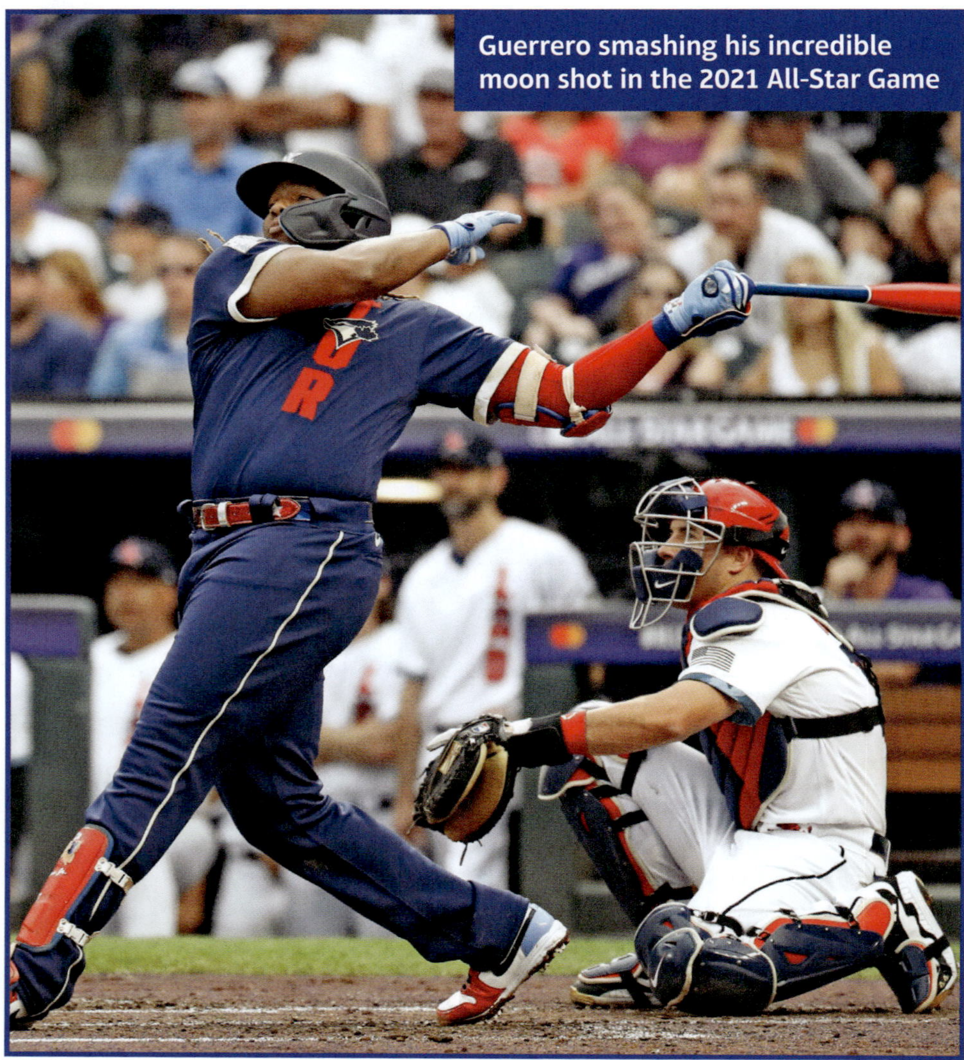

Guerrero shows off the 2021 All-Star MVP trophy. He won it after his amazing performance during the game.

special because Guerrero's father, Vladimir Guerrero Sr., was in the stands. In 2006, Vlad Sr. hit a home run in the All-Star Game. The Guerreros became the third father and son to both hit an All-Star home run.

"Dreams come true," Guerrero said in 2021. "Since I was a kid, I was thinking about this moment. I've worked all my life very hard and a lot of it is happening right now." Baseball's next big superstar was here.

CHAPTER 1

EARLY DAYS

Vladimir Guerrero Jr. was born on March 16, 1999, in Montreal, Quebec, Canada. His father played for the Montreal Expos. Vlad Jr.'s uncle Wilton Guerrero was also an MLB player. During the winter, Vlad Jr. lived with his mother, Riquelma Ramos, in the Dominican Republic. In the summer, he stayed with his dad in Canada or the US.

Vlad Jr. loved hanging out in the Expos dugout and meeting all the players. He was also well known around the team's clubhouse. His dad was one of the best hitters in baseball and a favorite of Montreal fans. In 2002, the Montreal crowd stood and cheered for Vlad Sr. As he stood on the field waving his cap, three-year-old Vlad Jr. trotted out in a kid-sized Expos uniform to join him.

Guerrero loved hanging out with the Expos team as a kid.

Vlad Sr. took off his hat. Then he told Vlad Jr. to take his off too. The crowd was still clapping, and the father and son waved to the fans together. A photographer took a now-iconic picture of them. Before long, Vlad Jr. decided he wanted to be in MLB like his dad.

Vlad Sr. set a high standard for Vlad Jr. to follow. He finished his career with 2,590 hits, 449 home runs, and nearly 1,500 RBIs. He retired in 2011 and joined the Baseball Hall of Fame in 2018.

Guerrero and his father wave their caps to the crowd in 2002.

Early on, Vlad Jr. set his sights on matching his father. "My goal is to be the same as him, or even better," he explained. With a lot of practice, Vlad Jr. closed in on his goal. By the time he turned 16 in 2015, he was one of the highest-rated prospects in baseball. The only question was which MLB team would sign him first.

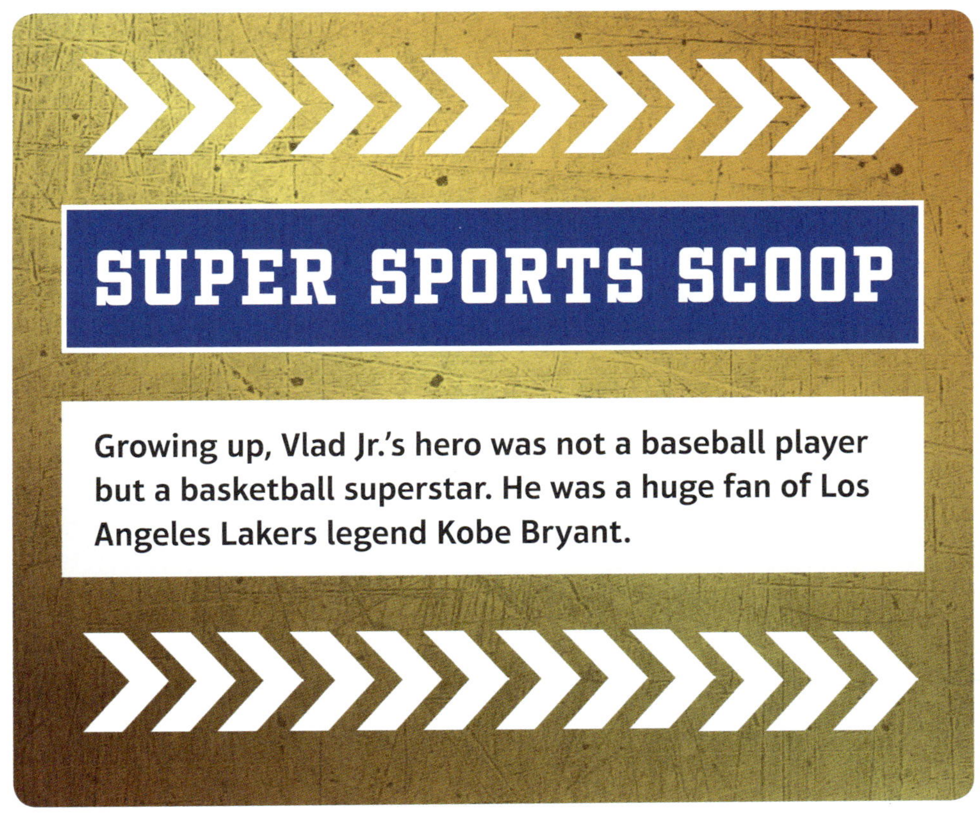

CHAPTER 2

YOUNG STAR

In July 2015, Guerrero signed a $3.9 million contract with the Toronto Blue Jays. The Blue Jays were excited to have a player from Canada on their roster. Their scouts had been watching Guerrero for over a year. They were impressed by his bat speed. It helped that Guerrero was a baseball player's son. Because he had spent so much time around baseball teams, he would know what to expect when he joined one.

Like most young players, Guerrero started out in the minor leagues. But he attracted more attention than most first-year players. Everywhere he went, Guerrero drew big crowds who were eager to see the game's next superstar. It didn't bother him. "Since I was a little kid, I [have] played with a lot of people watching me," he said. He just had to prove he could hit like his dad.

Rogers Centre in Toronto, Ontario, Canada, is the home stadium of the Toronto Blue Jays.

On June 23, 2016, Guerrero played in his first minor-league game. The next day, he hit his first home run. Over the next three seasons, Guerrero tore through the Blue Jays minor-league system. When the 2017 minor-league season ended, he returned to the Dominican Republic to play in the country's winter league. Blue Jays fans knew he would be a major leaguer.

Guerrero prepares to bat in 2016. Blue Jays fans were already excited to see him play more.

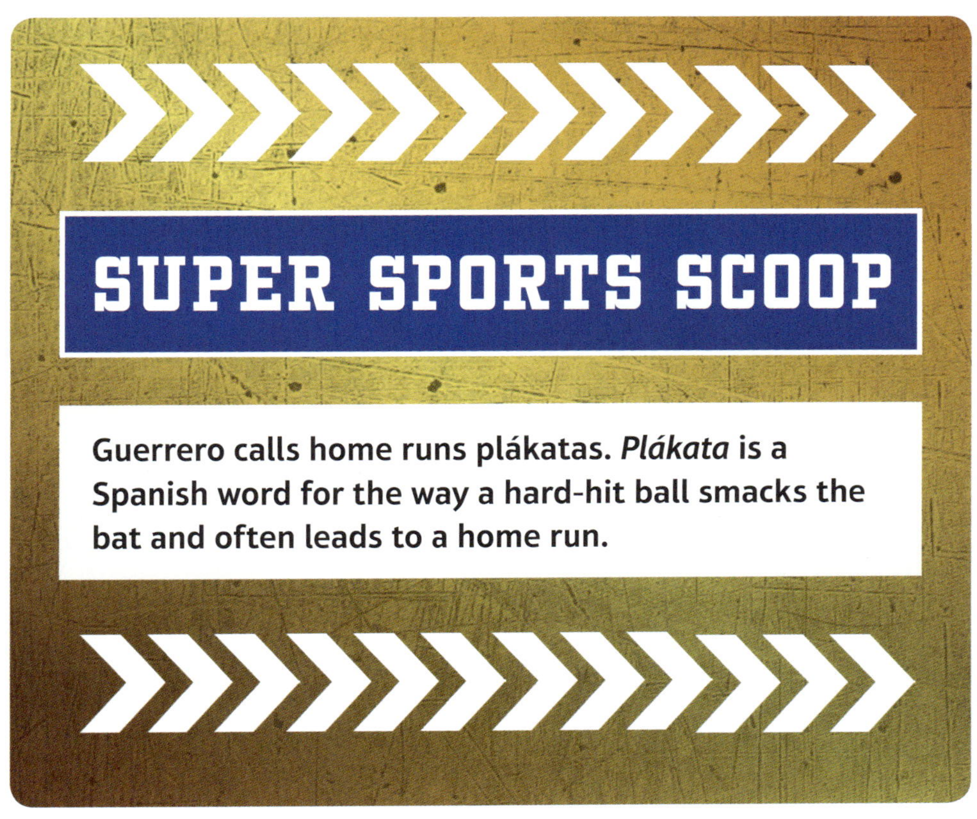

In July 2018, the Blue Jays announced that Guerrero was promoted to the Buffalo Bisons. He was one step away from MLB. To make it even more exciting, the news came just one day before his father joined the Baseball Hall of Fame. The family legacy was passing on from father to son.

MAJOR-LEAGUE VLAD

Barely a month into the 2019 season, the Blue Jays decided they couldn't keep Guerrero in the minor leagues any longer. He was doing so well that the team called him up to the major leagues. He played in his first MLB game on April 26, 2019. In the bottom of the ninth inning, Guerrero swatted the ball for his first major-league hit. A couple of weeks later, he hit his first home run on May 14, 2019. He was the youngest Blue Jays player ever to hit a home run.

Guerrero rounding the bases after his first MLB home run on May 14, 2019

Many young players have a hard time adjusting to life in MLB. But Guerrero had a secret weapon. His abuela, or grandma in English, Altagracia Alvino, lived with him and prepared his meals. Alvino cooked for a food stand in the Dominican Republic for many years, so she knew her way around a kitchen.

Guerrero talks to his abuela during batting practice. She is one of his biggest supporters.

Along with favorite meals like stewed chicken and goat or rice and beans, Guerrero's abuela dished out good advice. "She always tells me to respect the game and to respect my teammates," Guerrero said.

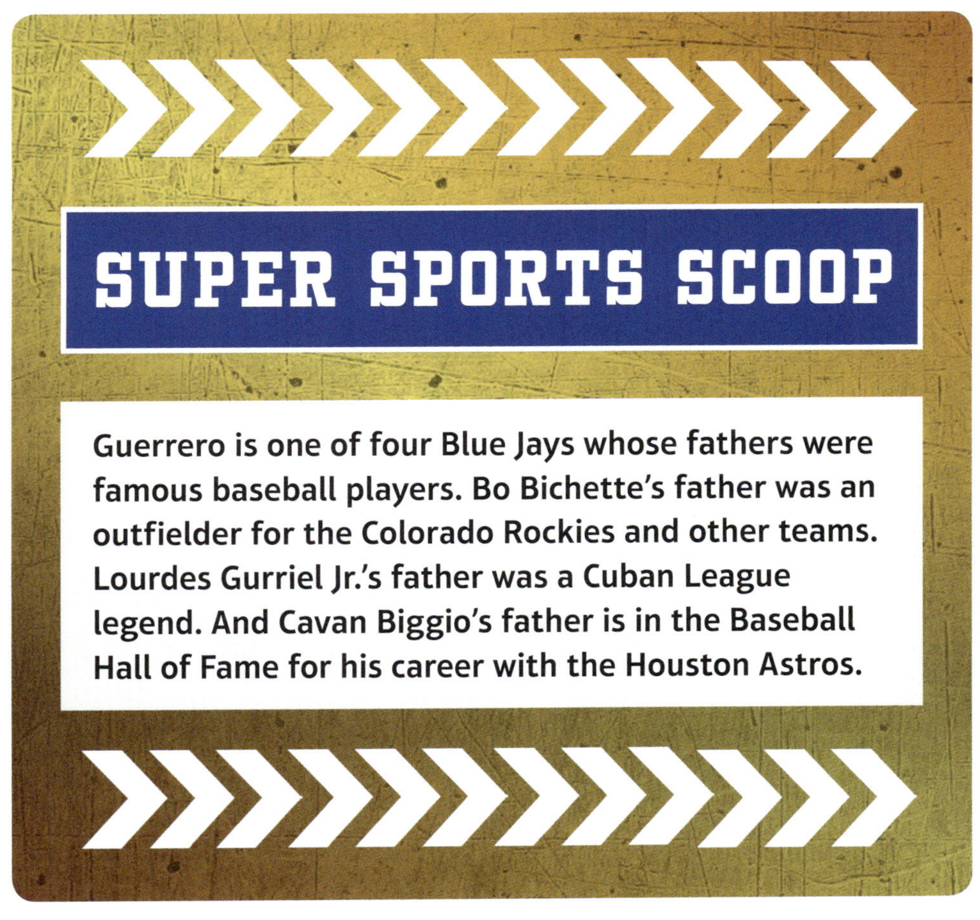

Every day at 11 a.m., Guerrero got up and packed the food his abuela had made for him that day. He brought it with him to Rogers Centre, the Blue Jays' home stadium, to share with his teammates. That made him very popular with other Blue Jays players.

Fueled by his abuela's cooking, Guerrero had a spectacular rookie season in Toronto. He slugged 15 homers with 69 RBIs. They were excellent stats for a first-year player. He also nearly won the Home Run Derby at the All-Star Game. Blue Jays fans looked forward to the next season. They hoped for a great season from their new star.

Guerrero bats in 2019. He played a skillful rookie season.

CHAPTER 4

THE NEXT SUPERSTAR

The 2020 baseball season was shortened to 60 games because of the COVID-19 pandemic. Many big events were canceled to help slow the spread of the disease. Even though the season was short, Guerrero still hit nine home runs. He also learned a new position after the Blue Jays moved him from third base to first base.

He had a strong season, but Guerrero wasn't satisfied. He sometimes felt tired during games, and he wasn't swinging the bat as quickly as he used to. He realized that he wasn't as fit as he wanted to be.

After the season, Guerrero changed his diet and fitness plan. He asked a personal trainer to help him design a new workout. Together they added stretching, weight lifting, and jumping exercises to his daily routine.

Guerrero's new fitness routine helped him become stronger and faster on the baseball field.

Guerrero stretching with teammates to prepare for a team training workout

Guerrero started drinking more water. He stopped snacking after dinner. And he asked his abuela for smaller portions of the meals she cooked for him. He also cut out fried food and sugar.

Guerrero lost 42 pounds (19 kg) by the start of the 2021 season. He was stronger and quicker, and he didn't get winded as easily. The new plan had worked.

The results showed on the field. Guerrero tied for the league lead with 48 home runs. He led MLB in runs scored. And he made a huge splash at the All-Star Game in Colorado with his amazing moon shot. Best of all, his fine play kept the Blue Jays in the running for the playoffs until the last week of the season. Although they fell short, clearly, the Blue Jays were one of the best young teams in the league.

Guerrero's play was even better during the 2021 season.

As the 2021 season wound down, fans in Toronto shouted "M-V-P! M-V-P!" They thought Guerrero was the league's MVP, or Most Valuable Player. And while Guerrero did not win the MVP award that year, he finished second in the voting. He had a new goal to shoot for in the years to come.

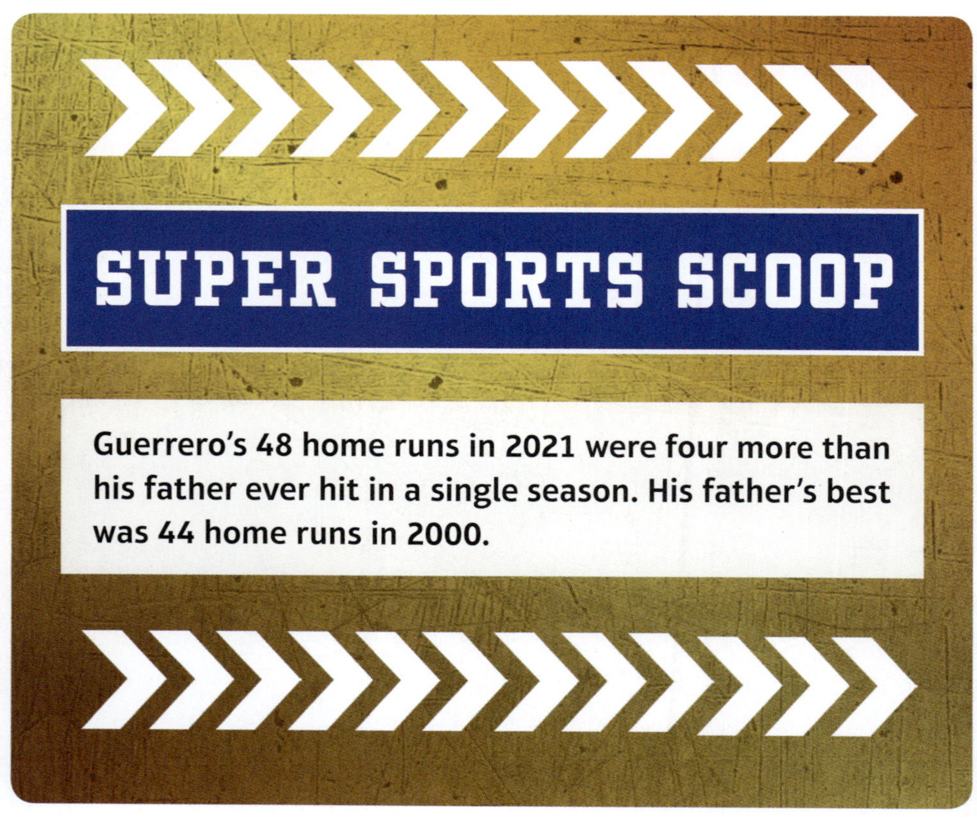

Guerrero smiles and has fun while he plays baseball.

VLADIMIR GUERRERO JR. CAREER STATS

GAMES PLAYED:
344

HOME RUNS:
72

BATTING AVERAGE:
.289

RUNS SCORED:
209

HITS:
372

RBIS:
213

Stats are accurate through the 2021 MLB season.

GLOSSARY

All-Star Game: a game played in the middle of each MLB season honoring that season's best players

dugout: a low shelter facing a baseball field where players sit

minor league: a pro baseball league that is not a major league

moon shot: a hit ball that travels a great distance

pandemic: a disease that spreads around the world

playoffs: a series of games played to decide a champion

prospect: a player who is likely to succeed at a higher level of play

RBI: short for run batted in, a run in baseball that is driven in by a batter

rookie: a first-year player

scout: a person who judges the skills of athletes

SOURCE NOTES

7 Mark Feinsand, "Vlad Youngest MVP after ASG HR for Ages," MLB.com, July 14, 2021, https://www.mlb.com/news/vladimir -guerrero-jr-2021-mlb-all-star-game-mvp.

11 Scott Stinson, "Blue Jays' Vladimir Guerrero Jr. Aiming to Top His Pop," *Toronto Sun*, March 13, 2017, https://torontosun.com /2017/03/13/blue-jays-vladimir-guerrero-jr-aiming-to-top-his -pop.

13 Jeff Blair, "Son of a Gun," Sportsnet, accessed April 20, 2022, https://www.sportsnet.ca/baseball/mlb/blue-jays-prospect -guerrero-jr-isnt-just-like-dad/.

19 James Wagner, "Abuela, Chef, Boss: Vladimir Guerrero Jr.'s Grandmother Feeds the Majors," *New York Times*, August 25, 2019, https://www.nytimes.com/2019/08/25/sports/baseball /abuela-chef-boss-vladimir-guerrero-jrs-grandmother-feeds -the-majors.html.

LEARN MORE

Baseball Facts for Kids
https://kids.kiddle.co/Baseball

Burrell, Dean. *Baseball Biographies for Kids: The Greatest Players from the 1960s to Today*. Emeryville, CA: Rockridge, 2020.

Doeden, Matt. *G.O.A.T. Baseball Teams*. Minneapolis: Lerner Publications, 2021.

Fishman, Jon M. *Baseball's G.O.A.T.: Babe Ruth, Mike Trout, and More*. Minneapolis: Lerner Publications, 2020.

MLB Kids
https://www.mlb.com/fans/kids

Toronto Blue Jays Official Site
https://www.mlb.com/bluejays

INDEX

PHOTO ACKNOWLEDGMENTS

Image credits: Ron Vesely/Getty Images, p. 4; AP Photo/Kyodo, p. 6; AP Photo/Jack Dempsey, p. 7; Cole Burston/Toronto Star/Getty Images, pp. 8, 12; AP Photo/Ryan Remiorz, p. 9; AP Photo/Paul Chiasson, p. 10; Freaktography/Shutterstock, p. 13; AP Photo/Brian Westerholt/Four Seam Images, p. 14; AP Photo/John Minchillo, p. 16; Robert Reiners/Getty Images, p. 17; Tom Szczerbowski/Getty Images, p. 18; AP Photo/Nathan Denette/The Canadian Press, p. 20; AP Photo/Tony Dejak, p. 21; Timothy T Ludwig/Getty Images, p. 22; AP Photo/Kathy Willens, p. 23; AP Photo/Steve Nesius/The Canadian Press, p. 24; Steven Crawford/Toronto Blue Jays/MLB Photos/Getty Images, p. 25; Daniel Shirey/MLB Photos/Getty Images, p. 27.

Cover image: AP Photo/Julian Avram/Icon Sportswire.